After The Games

Simon Mundy

After the Games

Simon Mundy

Calder Publications
London

First published in 2002
by Calder Publications UK Ltd.
51, The Cut, London SE1 8LF
and by Riverrun Press, New York
C/o Whitehurst And Clark Ravitan Industrial Park,
140, Newfield Ave.

ISBN 07145 43276

British Library Cataloguing in Publication Data is available
Library of Congress Cataloguing in Publication Data is available

Typeset by Alden Bookset
Printed by Alden Press

Contents

Blue Med

Sometimes the view is not enough,
The islands, the bobbing caps of early swimmers,
The ships lumbering past the headland
With its crest of concrete, its dance-hall
Gangsters, old libidos sunned on a shattered lido

Though the fishing boats with phallic prows
Come home late out of the mist trailing a flock
Of disappointed gulls screaming for warm guts,
Though the volley-ball girls
Have torsos tight enough for trampolines
Sometimes the view is not enough

Sometimes the view is not enough
For the men drowning off the breakwater,
Brisk yachts tacking snootily with idle crews,
For the garrison in a pointless fort, tourists
Posting look-out at the turret tops

When the under twenty-fives stretch
Untouched on the sand, comatose and soft
Wearing only a scowl of discouragement,
And the ice has melted in the warm gin
The flowers wilt in virgin-hard beds
Sometimes the view is not enough

Sometimes the view is not enough
For the beauty driving the bus in the heat
Of the morning, the toddler and her mother
Over-dressed and catholically pregnant
As the dust rises from the pavement

And away from the deceptive sea
Between the mountains, black slopes
Muddled in the sunset and the vines
In their autumn coats of auburn,
Curling yellow, when you are as handy as the moon
Sometimes the view is not enough.

Of Age

Now that you are all woman
Have watched yourself grow
Fill until others want to watch
And touch each part, caress its detail,
What will your answer be to the experimental
Ins and outs, false trails of love,
The competing promises?
Achievement for yourself
Or a family
Some rebellious girls of your own, perhaps?

The boys will never understand, will cop out,
Pursue the figure and the stroke at midnight,
The lager, the hooch,
The laughter with the lads,
Someone to take mother's place
Without the arguments.
For you first there is the dancing,
The beat and slap of it,
The heat that lifts the skin of the night.

Bombay

I

Why does the exchange of venues
So strange for both of us
Mean a secret imparted
A disembarkation into trust?

II

The road strafes Malabar Hill with traffic
Where gardens rise from the fetid pools
Step-cut terraces just alive with black leaves
Set as polite curtains netted in case we pry,
Tempt the vultures and the grey-necked crows
From the bones of the dead
Laid out as communion dinner
On marble tables closer to the sky.

III

What's in a winter wind, cleaning
The promenade in the face,
Buffing the coats of beggar monkeys?
A south-west kiss of spring in the Med
And an hour or two
When socks and jackets feel natural after all.

IV

Bedding down on plastic,
Thick cardboard if you're lucky,
Kicking a coconut husk in punctured dreams
The boys are nesting in the street dorm.
But where are the girls after eleven?
The night pretends to be a prudish chaperone.

V

The fallen flower
Flexing her petals on the red stone
Aspires to butterflydom
But her wings will rip too soon.

VI

I'm sorry, child,
You want to be paid,
Not rescued or praised.
Who pleads most need?
Who regrets?

VII

The insect that bit me
As I fought my nightmare alone
And you, wings folded inside the glass,
Have nothing in common
Except your deaths.

VIII

You are free, surely, to beg from
Pavement to pavement, catch a train,
Miss school, skip if you must on a wall top,
Watch the stars before the rains come,
Invent a new song after a successful hunt,
Gate-crash the smartest gates
In your one worn frock.
You are a bird
But the territorial rules are stricter than you thought,
There are lines in the street
Which only other birds can see.
Cross them
And more than the evening's profit will be lost.

IX

Was it the smell of roasted corn,
The hint of beheaded coconut in the air,
A perfume of taxi, horse and unwashed women,
The rattle of the monkey-boys' drums
Or sheer numbers that made me hurry for the gates?

X

Scattered husks,
Kernels of children
Sari sails
Sea made
Sun-white
Boats black
Bare brown
Almost there
Spinning chariots
Contrary - at a canter
Papa chappaty
Sotto voce. Car
Horns gutter all
Ghettos full blasted
Bingo and lime soda
Cricket tested
Stadium wedding
Without sex.

French Beach Bar

Lights however warm are too weak
To populate the beach on a cool night
When the fish prefer the full moon
To the lure, the fisherman circling,
A tractor-shark all shiny teeth and false gold

With no one else to serve
The waitress has time enough to charm,
Nobody rum to punch with the coast
This clear, the steaming Caribbean so far,
The great days buried with the resistance.

Cornish Beach

Behind the towels and the windbreaks
Underneath the junior surfboards
Between the cracked rocks

The sullen sand sticking inevitably
In human crevices,
The best of next season's beauties

Lark and grow self-conscious
Not old enough yet
To lie prone

Soaking up the stares
As hungrily as pores
Lap up the sun.

Times

If it had been the right time
He would have swept his cloak to the ground
Flourished it across a lake of puddles
He would have bought her roses to go with great
    champagne
Instead of the half-decent red, or better still
Have instructed a troop of waiters to appear
With operatic bouquets of rare and tender orchids,
The waiters themselves garlanded with jewels.

If it had been the right time
He would have swept her to an island beach
Where the sound of the sea washing clean the coral
Clinked cheerfully with that of different waiters
Bringing ice across the sand for the first
Cocktail of the evening, the start
Of a tequila night, listening out
For the splash and whoop of flying fish.

If it had been the right time
He would have loved her wholly, trumpeted
Her magnificence on the stages, the screens of all
    nations,
Eschewed all copyright on his valedictions
So that no-one should have been ignorant of beauty
That made Cleopatra seem little more than a sphinx
In desperate need of a radical nose job.

If it had been the right time
She would have filled his nights as he
Filled his glass, with no room for moderation, let alone
Modesty or abashed care for the bodily consequences.
They should have danced.

But, she implied with her averted eyes,
The tilt of her lips, the slight blush,
The right time would never come,
At least not for him,
And even the half-decent red
Was as good as he would get
Before the wrong time answered
That time was up.

Archives

In the shed are the old letters,
Many by the dead, some forgotten
One or two notes from the famous,
A card from Berlin as the wall came down,

The beginnings and the ends of love,
A few demands and thank yous,
Congratulations, important then,
For things I cannot remember doing,

Some are minor treasures,
Some archival embarrassments
Kept to give the rounded picture,
Castigations for not loving enough.

The ink is fresh, the paper dry,
The spiders have left the files alone
The love drained from the pages,
The crosses kiss for other men

Or impotent linger on their sides
To signal rest, in peace.

Summer Concert At Trolhaugen

Beyond the piano, the water
Purrs in the nocturnal sun,
Kissing the fjord warm for a lazy month
Easing the lyric melodies from the islands.

I want to turn and discover you
In the way the composer opened a new leaf of virgin
    manuscript.
I want to smile at you
Not the framed view across the inlet,

Mirror the stroke of a player's finger on the keys
But in these puritan days such freedom is unseemly
And instead my eyes caress the turn of your
    stockinged ankle
Savour the velvet on your crossed knee

The tiny foot, the fjord that leads from your hip
Nowhere that I can sail.
In this so little has changed,
A few years for us,

A hundred or so
Since the music flowed from the shed below
Great men wore whiskers of desire
And carried a comb of horn and silver.

Now I Wear A Suit

The train, Lausanne-Frasne

Now I wear a suit and sit in the expensive plastic trains
With the smart men,
The coiffured older women,
All scarves and gilded spectacles

TGV - try going vertically
Up the social ladder
With someone else paying for the assent,
The attitude, the altitude,

The continental aplomb,
The cosmo air
But it does not feel first class
Just class, old, older class

Never now a backpack or a student lover,
No lolling in the corridors
With a flask of dodgy thin wine
As we struggled

Through the mountains towards the Italian light
Stretching, inflating desire faster
Than our confident engine,
Now just so much scrap.

Recipe

Par-boiling would help the mandrake root, I thought,
With the addition of carrots,
Sweet potatoes pulled by hand without the help
Of a commandeered dog. I left out
The onions, thinking they would make the crying
    worse,
And tried more than the usual
Libation of old but decent Chianti,
Chianti because of some half-baked Italian memories
    of Mandragola.
I made the pastry extra tough and stoked
The Raeburn until it would have burnt a turkey.
A three hour visit to the pub, out of earshot, distracted,
Letting it get on with cooking,
Should have been enough.
Indeed when I returned
Things did seem quieter in the oven
Tempting as the stew smelt,
There seemed a chance that properly modest helpings
Would keep the bane in check.
She was a lusty root when I uncovered her.
I should have known mere cooking
Would not stop the screams.

Moving Out

And two days later the dead flies
Litter the carpet and carpet the sills,
There are no private drawers any more
For the family to invade, no secrets

Except those taken with me in my head,
More important than others will ever know,
Spread in pockets with holes, to be found
At a time when they will tip the balance,

The piper in the cathedral, the patch
Of earth on a Corsican hillside, the bare
Wall and cleared bed, the bathroom
Free of young perfume, could all have been the end

And two days later the flies are back,
The guests arrive, assume possession
Though I will possess them as they sleep, puncture
Dreams with spectral fingers until they come again.

Video Art

Dancing through the wind
In bathing cap and petticoat, the lithe one
With two fat ladies
Freed to undulate across concrete floors,
Block rusted windows jagged with glass

Through the wind that played with the bedroom door
Masking the hinge creaks, the nimble visitor
Who knelt and sought communion of a kind
But never prayed, never moved
Frozen by the bedside while the vision spun

The wind played underneath the petticoat
Its choreography undisciplined but beautifully
Rehearsed to reach its peak on the third night
In another theatre on a well-sprung forgiving stage
Doors shut against spectating strangers who interrupt
    the dream.

Entrance

They are two bow windows
Framing a door and I could
Slip between them almost
Unnoticed my fingers gently
Easing the handle down
Pressure enough to push
Open the panel and smiling
Allow some light to penetrate.

Ghost In The Dark

Above the short staircase in the dark
Outside the round bedroom
There hangs a small shapeless ghost
Darker than the air around it
Resisting the hand reaching for the light switch
Urging the door handle to recede.
Even in soft and shadow blended twilight
Her sounds compete with passing cars.
At night the ghost makes herself comfortable
Behind the door to the water tank
Blinking occasionally to keep awake
For your possible expedition downstairs to the loo.
    Feeling her is easy and though she is growing
    Less troublesome with age, she still coughs.

Old Park, Sunday Evening

The short autumn afternoon limped away
Along the paths between the park benches
Some green, some black under the lamps and damp
    from dying leaves
The lake was all blackening too, guarded by chestnut
    soldiers

It had been gentle sunshine when the father
    began to circle,
Rowing with steady hands, easing the blades around
    with confidence,
Son calmed by the rhythm, watching intently as sure
    strokes drove them
Across the brackish water, his Black Sea

Now it was truly dark but the oars dipped on
The repeating shore close enough for comfort
Distant enough for the thrill of deep uncharted water.
One pair of lovers had long since given up

Counting the circuits, the fretting birds,
The reluctant dogs called home in the dusk.
Their kisses had been transient
The stuff of familiar weekend duty.

Two seats down, a boy's mile up coast,
Others kissed differently, with the fire of exploration,
Founding colonies with lips
Discovering islands of plenty and priceless spice.

Which ship will voyage home first: the intrepid
      on the lake
Or the glorious conqueror of the new tropics,
Taurus and Leo - too far apart for
Earthly geographers, too close for priests?

And, North

And again you are not here
And the islands are not the ones I wanted
Full of warmth in the evening
And the stumble of the waves exhausted

And the wine has turned to beer
And the water to ice
The land Hibernian brown and worse
And a kiss would spin the map.

Helen - I

You must be sick of Troy
A city that you do not come from,
Sick of being away so long,
However splendid the gold
Or the view across the beach,

So long that now the battle lines
Are showing at the corners of your eyes
Along with the glitter,
Sick of the beauty cage though
Frightened its bars might break,

Sick of the boy that caged you,
Passable enough at the time and worth
Annoying the immortal competition for
But rather wet now, given the calibre
Of those fighting men from home

Who have come smiling after you,
Squandering their honour and their harvest.
You must be sick of Troy
Even though they add it to your name.
What wouldn't you give for a fling?

Helen - II

No

Once you were a great beauty of Europe
Tall and perfect

Now you are just another woman
Dressed like the girl who said no

Always no
So the asking dwindled

The long secure years
Will be the years of being alone.

Helen - III

Rescues

And when you look back over these years
Remember the pleasure you gave,
The rescues, so quick and profound, from fear
Only you could see and touch away into the mercenary
    night,

Loneliness from shared houses bereft of passion,
Minds tortured by the landscape of their faces,
The pits and canyons, livid rouge,
Wretched symmetry and scabrous hair.

Fear of unproven youth too nervous to function
Or outdated machinery that has lain
Pathetic and half-abandoned under faded covers
Spotted with the must of antiquity.

All of these you have gripped and tasted,
Sent preening exultantly on their way,
For they have bought a potion from you,
A tincture of Aphrodite, fresh distilled.

Helen - IV

Motion Sickness

Even if the wine was everything
Love was plundered to exhaustion,

Even if wallets never emptied
Teams won alternate matches,

Women would claim it was betrayal
And men would not be satisfied.

Love Shopping

On the Via Garibaldi the trim lovers ambled andante
So different from the arguing pair
At the Café Paris table in the middle of the street
Or those that had come separately to breakfast
Sharing only a spoon to stir further
And parted silently after a yoghurt,

The trim lovers meandered before the windows
Steering each other across the street in alternate sweeps
Between jackets, accessories,
Shoes and the underwear of adventure.

The trouble only surfaced halfway down the Via Roma
Where the arcades split, cafés and shops on either side.
There was no time to consider both avenues
No time to satisfy both desires

To manipulate for victory,
To wear the other down with tears
Persuade with flattery,
Trade favours for the future.
One shopped, one sulked
And love was sullied for the day.

Clothes

I

The black leather
Shines too new
Absurdly stern
At twenty
A pedal biker
With kindly eyes
Come hither lips
And never never zips.

II

The river is low
As you crouch
On the shingle
Black boots, long white neck,
Checked blue linking
Eyes and jeans and a smile
That cannot quite forgive.

III

Oh! That cotton calico
Could have lost its opacity
Left you for the magnolia wall,
The jeans, too dark for a cowgirl,
Fallen to the washed pine floor
Ashamed to be hiding
Five sculpted treasures
And the soft green of confident eyes
Be redeemed, reduced
To loving size
For in that pose of perfect bones
Consistent angles
Rampaged chemical decline.

IV

It was a chilly April
Too much for hands
To be out of pocket
Grey scarf unwound
Or full bleached skirt
Hitched to offer me
The legs and beyond
Of a consummating summer.

V

The long loose dress
Was a gloomy one
For Florentine gardens
In temperate spring,
Small white flowers
Sprinkled but making
Little cheery impression.
Face as droopy
As the Indian silver earrings,
You struggled with
Renaissance questions.
Why were you there,
Was bringing you significant?

VI

You had a figure
That was furiously female,
Called male fingers
To all its clefts and corners
But nothing peeks
From the roll-neck
Under cable-knit
Or a dozen years
Beneath a shroud.

Anti The Cyclone

I wish one day you'd stop raining,
Stop feeding me with constant streams,
Stop washing away my fragile sandstone,
My gargoyles and filigree, my cultivated sins,
Stop marooning ancient burial mounds
Standing fiercely on my flood plain,
Stop sweeping the rubbish, stinking nicely,
Down protesting drains and out to sea,
Stop washing my already washed linen,
Laundering it of intimate traces,
Stop bringing seeds to life that had lain
Happily dormant for a season or two,
Stop offering me rainbows against indigo skies
So much more arresting than the facing light,
Stop wetting my skin, clothes, hair, socks,
My bedding and leading, my pots and plans,
Stop drenching my evening calm,
Stop arriving from the clouds with fresh storms,
I wish you'd stop raining and stay to enjoy the sun.

Neptune Becalmed

What pleasure can there be at the fountain?
Every delight is denied
Except the sound
Of water running over stones
So vulgar they debase those who sit
And watch and toss away their difference
Over the shoulder like salt in the eye of the devil
Fifty lire to the state of Rome
No sex, no dancing by the water
Brief relief for abused feet but no dipping
From a white marble bench
Gaze at Neptune
Becalmed ten miles from the sea
Nothing on show is really available
Nothing offered to the fountain will be returned.

Siesta 1699
(outside Vittoria)

Never, never quiet in the Palace.
Servants fussed tables into place
Worried dishes for later, hurried meat,
Practicing musicians competed with performing birds
And lost. In the private rooms the wind annoyed duennas
Dons divested peasant girls under the afternoon sun

Tourists pretended to be pilgrims then
Looking for a cheap night just passing towards
   Santiago,
Craving cold wine in the high plains
With a flourished letter full of papal bull.
The Palace creaked too much
For an indecent unzipped snooze.

Bar Code

There are three promises to be turned down
At the end of a busy evening
For the barmaid in black

Three men who will wait till the others leave
To beg a little, lure her from the bicycle
Each convinced that tonight will be their turn

The choice at the closing hour
Is between beer, wine and orange juice
Spread evenly along the bar

It is a process of attrition
With no victory for the drunk
No satisfaction for the sober

For she smiles, closes the money drawer
Begins the final wash routine of glasses
And, squeezing the hand of each, declines.

At A Film,
With the Person On Screen Sitting In Front Of Me

Against the restless image, back immobile
So moving, loud in spectating silence
Alive composure, balance perfect
Tiny reality against yourself on the great screen,
Down here reduced to lifeless grey and beige,

Up above in radiance, black, red and gold
And when the scene paraded on, replacing you
With old stock, landscapes you had never seen,
There you sat, hair drifting, too far away for scent,
A slight occasional tilt of the neck, no more.

All around they shuffled and adjusted, laughed
Crossing and recrossing legs as though
They were your piano fingers
Playing about you in the middle register,
Immaculate fulcrum, automatic poise.

Light came to the screen, a picnic,
I could see you vividly again and waited
For the last page of script, the credits,
The shock of your final chord, cue
For a stretch and the real beginning.

The Candidate

The rear window misted up under the downpour,
Slogans were rendered unreadable and the bird
    of Victory
Grounded for the afternoon.
Poring over the canvass cards, running ink,
Supportive promises and probables and ancient hatreds
Merging harmlessly into sodden discontent,

The candidate cried a little. Perhaps it was only rain
Finding a new course down creases under her eyes
That never showed in studio shots,
Crying for rest, not just sleep,
For an end to the terror grip on the neck,
Fear of a failing smile, a daggered handshake,

Dragging home muddy from a field of surly opponents
For a change of clothes, shoes, knickers, a dab
Of make-up never needed before these weeks,
A change of companion, less sympathy,
An agent without slick grey hair and a malaprop mouth,
For it to be over, to lie beside an honest man.

From Bierbeek, 1999

War is distant and only three days old
Banished from fertile Flanders in the weak March sun

At the edge of the trim grass
East of the abandoned trenches

Fresh with Spring
Wars of neighbours building steel fences

Far south burning children under the eaves
Candles for defeated ancestors

A new roof is red
And pitted concrete is redeemed with white.

Breaking Ground

At the corner of the football field
A house is soon to stand
A permanent linesman,
Flag raised for offside,

With a grandstand view
Of the humble tin shed behind home goal
Set high above the centre circle
Camera perfect for playing panorama

Spotting the ball heaved into river touch
Armchair managers kindle six yard memories
As they strike a match for winter fire.
Will the name fixed in iron on red bungalow

Reflect those glories
Or the sheep and foxes that sweep across the pitch
Except on Saturdays from three till five?
Perhaps enshrine young radiance

In the farmer's daughter pacing out the plot
Commemorate the old man who at eighty-two
Mowed the meadow before each game
Collected money at the rusting gate

Tom's House, Toll House, Fox Field, Arrow View,
Tŷ Donna, Maes Goal, Plas Neuadd.

Helsinki, November

Shivering in the ulcerated landscape
Caught between the acid forest
And the sea as it turns to land
Under the bitter gasp of the first snow

There is nothing of Wales here
In the futile chill of the island barracks
The slap of the Arctic wind
The clean designs embracing razor lives

There is nothing of Wales here
But in the lazy rumble of the language
Unpopular enough to be private
In the babble of greater Europe

In the blessed absence of aristocracy
The proud modesty of the towns
The amplitude of beer and womanhood
Wales would feel at home.

Preludes

I

Love is tolerant - of spring, the old spring
Which complains with tortured propriety,
Tolerant towards narrowness forcing
Petrified sleep or else a fast fall
(sometimes only inches, sometimes half
a fathom), of walls that amplify
And the imperfections of first morning
Love is tolerant and each soon wanes
Together in autumn camouflage.

II

Soft black, like curtains in the wings
That part without a rustle, letting
Hamlet offstage for the final release
Like sable brushed the wrong way to show
A glimpse of hide. Cast memories not
Cast iron or the smudge of ingrained coal.

III

The turbulence of spots betrays the anger of the sun
Bilious fury at the mismatch, cold gas against hot,
The agony of aborted fusion. How long did it take
For the eruptions to subside, the fetid flares to stop
Reaching impotently, never quite far enough into
    the night?

IV

Whenever the power jet, *le jadeau*, reaches
Asking questions I reach further, higher, seeking
Answers. Showers confuse the skin until it knows
Barely which is running water, which is justly
Wet and wonders if it will always be turned
On as easily as the restless water, fierce
But rarely constant, can be made to stop.

Postludes

I

Coiled all day from the heat of the sun
From the heart-stretching heat of the night
At the limit of the well as I plunged
Another python tensed against the first blow
Recoiled for the second, picking its hour
To unfurl to effect which it hoped
Would devastate time after my time.

II

The clarinet was not autumnal
Like Brahms and the red was the new red
Of April's bright redcurrant flowers
Not of apples bedded down in straw
Trying to stay fresh through the winter
But all red fades and the grip of lips
The tight embouchure slackens around
The reed and the clarinet turns sour.

III

Chastisement for broken chastity,
Mild pain for mildly induced pleasure
The warm anticipated slipstream
High in the summer night, the whispered
Cry for a demonstration of trust
Now, sharp, sudden and reliable
A slipper changed for a sturdy boot.

IV

Which, then, is later more important,
The speed, the occasional flurry,
The pleasure of all our hours forced
Into minutes, of months into that
Pair of days, brisk and impetuous,
Or the comfort of many returns?

V

Hold tight in case one night I slip in,
Breaking the window, the old pane
Of opportunity, the rhythm
That haunts our familiar old game
Hold tight in case far sudden sleep turns
Pleasure into a ghost before you
Have had the chance to give him a name.

VI

By now everything should have been smashed
The wine cups that never held enough
Wine to pour in libation, to spill
After dancing, hour after late hour
On the carnival sheets - or the mug
Muddy brown from which coffee never
Tasted quite right in the cold of a
Mist-strewn distant Cambridge morning.

VII

The afternoon was warm and the leaves
Were soft against the back, a needle
Or two pricked as a sharp memory
Of the woods above, counterpanes
To you the duvet, you on your way.

VIII

Bare on the bare floor squatting below
Three excited glaciers in the rain
Beside the bed frame, the used rough bed
In the tourist warm dry log cabin
A dog, a bitch, howled with wet pleasure
Loudly and deeply for the last time.

IX

At five in the morning the curtain
Parted, eyes dropped in hope without shame
And the sun that rose was not the same
Girl's sun that had lit the bloodless bed
Or coped till now with desperation.

X

When I was a boy sometimes the toys
That I loved most were the broken ones
Some parts missing, others slightly bent
So that the torn and brittle edges
Hard, sharp inside, caught me by surprise,
There was blood and crying but the toy
Was kept safe from the charity box.

XI

Like a kettle slow to start and quick
To boil over with a rising shriek,
The spring of a mousetrap touched too soon,
Wasted while its prey enjoys the meal,
Better to reset and start again
Before torpor claims the afternoon.

XII

For girls of twelve from the smarter towns
Pony trekking can open the eyes
The bridlepath is strewn with boulders
Behind windows, in fields and hay barns
Animals are pleased to illustrate
Biology outside the classroom.

XIII

The beak on a two-headed eagle
Bites however careful the approach
It nips and coos with ruffled pleasure
Front and back, talons splayed and gleaming
The eagle hoods its eyes and dares you
To chuck the feathers beneath each chin.

XIV

The tears in the night were one-sided,
Surprise and relief and nostalgia,
Though knowing you they were tears of shame
And fury was never far away.
Nonetheless it was a trivial end
To ten fond years and all those pages.

XV

When I saw there was an obstacle
Transparent but all enveloping
It seemed my mission could not develop
With any finesse or subtlety
But she knew I had to start somewhere
That room was as good as another
Any black cloth could be moved at will.

XVI

Across town the party was on its way
Champagne on ice, whisky dusted off
The words of Auld Lang Syne researched
In the lonely hours before midnight
There was a taste of perfect solace
Anticipating the bacchanal
As others hesitated until
The active hour when the year had died.

XVII

A potato is best filled when split
Baked ripe and dripping with the creamy
Gloss of hot butter, its flesh worked free
Saturated with the tang of salt
The gasp of pepper, cayenne and black
And added at the perfect moment
A ramekin of expensive roe.

XVIII

Now take the texture of a balloon
Pushing for the warp and give of it
Stroking until the skin screeches
Rubbing it fiercely against soft wool
So hair follows the rising rubber
Watch the bump and slap of two balloons
Filled with liquid and thrown together
Pushed and stroked and rubbed until they burst.

XIX

After the tea and other soothing drinks
Had been cleared away from around us
There were a few standing ends and odds
About the room needing attention
From a pair of warm and willing hands
Clever with damp cloth, brush and timing.

XX

The dark sound could never be the wind
For the northern night for once was still
The sea compliant under the moon
The low nocturnal cry of welcome
From the rocks held no edge of terror
Pleading, surely, for if beast it was,
It lay thin and waited to be fed.

XXI

The whole speech was forgotten because
The cloth at both ends of the table
Was wet, wetter than it should have been,
And later, when it came to the point
With the rich scented water spreading
None of the rhetoric quite rang true,
Answers were not the ones we wanted
Grazing soft against the raw edges
Without the tumult of slipping in.

XXII

Waves undulated against my back
And, discovering a tiny cave,
I pressed on, in, pushing the water,
Squeezed by the sides along the whole length,
Conscious of the cliff, hard rock, above,
Listening for the cry of the sea birds
High, high on the current, the storm wind
Waiting for the wrack of the low tide,
The soft creatures crawling from the cave.

XXIII

There were tears after the rocking chair,
Quiet tears with no faith in the future,
So much waiting, such fleeting reward,
The easy motion, locomotive,
May never bring that sweet calm again,
Banish fears with a whispered amen.

XXIV

Well used would have been the kinder phrase
But grubby grey and tattered fringes
Explains the sad state of all cloth
That lay forlornly about that house
On banisters, stairs and unswept floors
Like worn out lovers or sodden ropes
Flapping and slapping against a flag pole
Empty at a sullen stormy dawn.

XXV

As the fan split apart with a black
Flamenco flash streaked with carmen red
Rhythms crossed and surged in complex flame
Striking white sparks with heat-tempered steel
The blaze rose with the moon in the hills,
The city threw open its windows
To catch the howl rising from the pyre.

Among Vineyards

Is it illegitimate to dream
Of you now
Naked on the bleached grass
In Gascony
Knees pulled high and wide
Among vineyards
Pressing grapes, your breasts
For the red juice
As I press against your picture
In Rioja
And the wind sighs that there is nothing
Innocent still of use
Nothing platonic except the guests
Forecast in the cards
Nothing to make me stay outside
Especially matrimony
No argument to make me pass
Or hear that vow
Until I have made a torrent of your stream.

As Sudden

As sudden
As the moment when the birds leave together
Abandoning bread in the calm lake water,
Her change began

A whole fresh plumage pushing out
The old feathers, the dull grey,
The dowdy cygnet beige

It was still early evening,
The carnivores were hardly stretching
For the night's stalk and kill
They sat about, preening here and picking there,
Watching things with lazy interest,
No story yet,
No hurt contemplated.

Tonight though they would wait
And wait
Never come

They saw the change instead, the slither
From one life to the next, the slow
Recovery

It began like the ravaged earth
Under benign spring stars
Old tears were lost in silk brushed with silver
The rush of fear became gliding water
It only took a gentle paddle to speed away
Laughter shaking from the teal as they left
The snapping dogs so far below
The sea was crossed without a storm

About her face the lines of today's sorrow
Eased into tomorrow's beaming sun
And from that evening's alteration
There's a rebirth now
A shining soon.

28 October 1998

When Glen first went up it was another day,
As I was eight, of spam and tyranny,
Of music opening, of girls and maths
Equally sought, equally incomprehensible

The poet, not a laureate then, who went up
Today faster than his hunted hare or waterfall,
Beating Glen this time for all time,
Ascending without a flash at speeds

That left shuttles lumbering well before orbit,
Still believed American love could triumph
Through the flame and mingled gases
To forge a verse from nature shaped by man

And bring us to our shattered senses;
Now Glen tests age as the other tests death
Together circling the earth, monitoring
The slightest twinge of heart and soul,

The contacts with gods and minor deities
Both have touched before and through them all
The flood waters rose in the borderlands,
The wine was kissed with words and deeds.

Falstaff in Amsterdam

Happy in their congregation
The twenty-somethings, some two to a stool
Taste union in the late spring sun
The first evening for sitting out,
Sorting out the new loves from the old

Alone now, spearing olives at the bar
Much older, of course, than they can imagine,
The patina on the walls, the heart,
The sticky bar, chipped boards, unreliable erection,
The barely visible mural of a landscape,
Real once, now a fairy tale

Between the beer pullers and the beer swillers
There is cross and counter-cross
Kiss, the belonging caress
Pistol and the rest
Young Bartolph, so in charge of bills and orders,
Alice, Jet and Saskia, briskly beautiful
As they polish and carry the trays,
Floating cascades of glasses
The spume of spilled ale

There is nothing left to say
Falstaff has no jokes they want to hear
No wisdom to swat imperfect lines
Nothing to demand a parry and riposte
The ancient verbals when there was
An erotic world to conquer among friends

Pay the bill, old man
And be grateful
For the distracted wave goodbye.

Book

The Doctor's murder
Small town
In the hills

North Carolina
Carson's house
The great view

The party
At the house
In the hills

Looking at three states
And the wife
With the knife.

After The Games

I left the games with no medals
Or assurances of a place with the team
For next year; umpire I expect,
Raising a doleful finger
On behaviour that merited indulgence
Issuing judgements indoors

From an uneasy perch
Half way up the wall
Staring down on my descendants
Not with the stern robes of authority,
The senator, the professor of immoral philosophy

But with impatience, aged three
From my father's knee pretending to read
Wisdom from an orange book
It's title blanked out in flecks of paint.

I am impatient now for the games,
New games to start again.